Inside Perceptions

Inside Perceptions

Carol A. Boyd

VANTAGE PRESS
New York

Photography:

Cover Photo: Gil Bailey; *The Camera's Eyee,* Nashville, Tennessee
Ocean Photo: Daniel K. Nolly, Los Angeles, California
Romance Photo: Deacon W.T. Martin, Indianapolis, Indiana
Sunset Photo: Julia Y. Boyd, Nashville, Tennessee

Cover design by Susan Thomas

FIRST EDITION

All rights reserved, including the right of
reproduction in whole or in part in any form.

Copyright © 2004 by Carol A. Boyd

Published by Vantage Press, Inc.
516 West 34th Street, New York, New York 10001

Manufactured in the United States of America
ISBN: 0-533-14486-8

Library of Congress Catalog Card No.: 2002095914

0 9 8 7 6 5 4 3 2 1

This book is dedicated with deep love and affection to the memory of Melvin, my loving husband, who was for forty-two years my best friend and lifetime partner. Without his love and support, this book would not be possible.

And to

All of the readers who love the beauty and imagery of poetry.

Contents

Foreword	xi
Acknowledgments	xiii
Welcome to My Heart	1

I. Friendship and Happiness

I Think You Are Really Great	5
I'll Lend You an Ear	6
Hope of Height	7
This Could Be Your Life	8
Get Up, My Friend	9
I Thought I Could Do It	10
Today Is Here Right Now	11
Oh, Celebrate with Me	12
Dream Traveling	13
Color Me Happy	14

II. Inspirations of Nature

From the Depths of Splendor	19
I Ride the Deep	21
Water Symphony	22
I Know the Storm Is Nigh	23
The Wonder of Color	24
In the Whisper of Sundown	25
Speak to Me Softly	26

III. Romance and Love

Our Eternal Love	31
Candlelight and You	32
By the Fireside of Love	33
I Wish You Love	34
So Is My Love for Thee	35
Intoxicated Over You	36
The Way I Love You	37

IV. Spiritual Insights

Thy Will, O Lord, Be Done	41
Let Excellence Reign	42
Launch Out	43
Beyond the Horizon	44
Someday	45
Memories, They Are the Dreams	46
Think on These Things	47
Cords of Love	48
Open Mine Eyes	49
O God, Your Love Is Constant	50
May God Bless All His Children	51
Cherish the Children	52
Gifts of Life	53
I'm Black But Comely	55
I Fell Right into Your Grace	57
Looking for God	58
The Fool	59
The Prodigal	60
The Crying Heart	61
Your Honor	63
Unequaled	64
On the Rampage	65

The Dream	66
Rich Man—Poor Man	68
I've Also Cried Rivers of Joy	70

V. In Loving Memory
Out of the Waters	73
Drifting Out to Sea	75
I'll Always Love You, Mama	76
Like a Dream	77

Foreword

My mother, Carol Boyd, has been a writer for twenty-nine years. She was first inspired to write in 1974 as she sat and listened to my father minister the word of God. It was not until many years later that she realized she had a gift from God, and she began to record her thoughts.

Her poems reflect her experiences in life and a deep devotion for the spiritual things of God. She has a sense of romanticism and writes straight from her heart about love, friendships, and happiness. She has a sincere appreciation for God's magnificent creation and writes about the beauty of flowers, the mountainside, and the sunset. She has a fond love for water and writes profoundly about the ocean.

The last four poems in this book are tributes, and reflect her love, devotion, and passion for her family.

Inside Perceptions is a book to encourage, motivate and inspire the heart. Carol Boyd is proud and eager to share her first publication with you.

Toyia C. Mundy
Nashville, Tennessee

Acknowledgments

I thank God my Creator, for giving to me the gift for writing poetry.

After being traumatized by losing my husband a few months ago, the desire to finish my book quickly diminished, still, the love he gave to me continues to support me through my difficult times. Through months of struggling and shedding many tears, God has given me the strength to complete what He has given me, to share with the many readers my first publication, *Inside Perceptions*.

To my sons and daughters, Melvin, Michael, Toyia, Marsha, Myron, Monica, and Mark, and to all of my grandchildren, I love you. Many thanks for your contributions toward this manuscript. Thank you, Monica, for the layout and design, and above all, your patience as you worked untiringly to help me.

I sincerely thank Elaine Prather for her willing spirit, and her patience while typing, and retyping drafts of this manuscript in the early stages of preparation.

To my family and many friends who believed in me. You taught me the true meaning of encouragement and support.

Inside Perceptions

Welcome to My Heart

Welcome to my heart, dear friend
And please receive my love.
The thought to touch your life,
Comes straight from up above.

I share with you these dreams
I muse within my intellect,
So read me now and read me well.
These words shall be a gift.

Welcome to the page I'm on.
It is open, so please read
The thoughts I have and the way I feel;
Come in and go with me.

I've opened up my heart to you,
I'm sure you will find a pearl.
Welcome to my heart, dear friend,
Welcome to my world.

I

Friendship and Happiness

I Think You Are Really Great

This is what I think of you, my friend,
I think you are really great.
Sometimes you feel like crying,
But you tell the tears to wait.

You strive to keep on going;
You seem to never stop.
Like a steady mountain climber,
You are bound to reach the top.

You seem to always want to share,
And not just with a few.
You give a lot to others, friend;
It's coming back to you.

This is what I think of you, my friend,
I think you are really great.
You have courage undefeated and
Strength of will that just won't break.

So, friend, just hang on in there,
For the fight is not over yet.
You will be declared a winner,
So why worry and why fret?

I'll Lend You an Ear

I'll lend you an ear and it won't cost a thing,
Perhaps in a while you might even sing.
Your troubles are buried deep down inside,
So bring them on out and face the sunshine.

There is a way, and yes, there is hope,
Whatever the problem, I know you can cope.
So pour out your heart, go ahead if you dare.
I'll give you some time, I've moments to spare.

You just need some cheer and a very warm smile,
I'll listen and you talk, for it may take awhile.
You won't be a bother, I promise you that,
I'll listen and you talk, just give me the facts.

I'll lend you an ear, say, what is that sound?
There's a change in your tone, and speech so profound.
You smile and laugh, your eyes, how they gleam,
Is that melody new? My, how you sing!

Hope of Height

You came unclothed, into this world
To be clothed with righteousness,
And gallantly climb to reach the mark
For the prize of the high call in Jesus!

You dare to venture where great men have,
Walking the holy highway!
Love is your staircase to higher heights,
Look up, and not away.

Be proud walking onward, and upward too.
Hold your head high with dignity.
Climb higher and higher until troubles seem
To vanish like each passing day.

Be secure in God's love and protection always,
Don't give up for your crown yet awaits,
For soon you'll be there at the very top,
The bliss of unending day.

This Could Be Your Life

This is your life, oh miserable man,
Weak and helpless you can't even stand all
The problems, pressures, and tension life brings,
You're shattered by sin and wickedness of men.
You struggle and grasp for things out of reach,
You stumble, you fall, you cry, "Help me please".

You're sowing and reaping, you sink in despair,
You want a way out; doesn't anyone care?
This could be your life, oh, man, great or small,
You don't have to stumble, and you don't have to fall.
God's word has shown what is required of thee;
To walk humbly before God, meek and lowly.

Jesus the way, the truth, and the life
Is the very best way, this could be your life;
Singing and praying and walking in light;
No grasping in darkness and blindness of night;
Living each day and striving for right;
This is the first day of the rest of your life.

Get Up, My Friend

Get up, my friend, and come take my hand,
I'll walk with you in a weary land.
Don't sit and stare and heave a sigh;
Time has a way of passing you by.

Get up, my friend, just don't sit by the way,
There is work to do, no time for delay.
Can't you hear the cries of the hungry and poor?
It sounds like thunder—I can't take any more!

Get up, my friend, we have mountains to climb,
We have rivers to cross that are deep and wide.
We have miles to walk to accomplish our goal.
Look at the world with the eyes of your soul.

Get up, my friend, for the day is not done;
I'll walk with you and we will be as one.
United together we can launch our plan
And keep on believing there is hope for man.

I Thought I Could Do It

I thought I could do it; make a contribution,
In a world filled with so much pollution.
I could ponder poverty and chaos in the land,
Or decide to get up and lend a helping hand.

Oh, I'm just one person, it's a fact I know, but
In the volume of learning I've room to grow.
I'm quite alert to the situation of
Perilous times in a shaky nation.

The nation lacks strength and is short on perfection,
But her strongest link is love's connection.
It's the key to all hearts that unlocks the door,
That opens its home to the rich and the poor.

I thought I could do it; spread love all around,
Draw smiles on some faces, and erase a few frowns.
Oh, I'm just one person, so what can I do?
Why don't you join me? One and one make two.

Today Is Here Right Now

Tomorrow is so close, my friend;
But today is here right now.
You have great treasures in this life,
But you're wondering where, and how.

Opportunity is just around the bend,
And yet you would hesitate, for
You think that you have plenty of time
And so you procrastinate.

Tomorrow is so close, my friend,
And yet it may never come.
Welcome happily the open door.
Hurry in, for it will soon close.

Today becomes yesterday, past and gone,
With things you wish you had done,
But the door will close and not open again,
And the key will not be found.

Your hopes and dreams you must claim today
And yet, pushing through is the crowd.
Tomorrow is so close, my friend,
But today is here right now.

Oh, Celebrate with Me

Oh, celebrate and dine with me,
Drink up this cup of joy;
Rejoice with them who will rejoice,
So says the Word of God.

Be fully dressed tonight, my friend,
Adorn a cheerful smile.
Oh, deck thyself with happiness
And wear it for a while.

Oh, gird thyself with gladness,
Take up a song of praise.
Great is the faithfulness of God
He gives to us this day.

His banner over us is love
And the beauty that we see.
This banquet is a time of joy.
Oh, celebrate with me!

Dream Traveling

Let me fly away to distant places,
Golden days and happy faces;
Kiss floating clouds in misty skies
And rise to where the sun always shines.

Let me leave the earth and touch the sky,
Forsaking weary days and nights.
The wind becomes my traveling path,
Its invisible strength, a mysterious fact.

A million thoughts pass through my mind;
I'm near to God in a frame called time.
Is it fact, fantasy, or physical whim?
All things are real when I think of Him.

I gaze out of the window in this flying machine,
And catch the horizon just over the wing;
Red, pink, then a bright golden hue,
All seem to blend into a sky of blue.

I'm back again down on the ground
For just a while, then I'm moving on
To the same destiny of distant places;
Golden days and happy faces.

Color Me Happy

Color me happy and color me joy
In a pleasant memory;
With strength I now my wits employ
Such sweet serenity.

Color me happy and color me joy
In rays of shining light.
I look not at night, nor at the dark,
I see the light of peace in my mind.

Color me handfuls of love, bottled up
And rivers of sweet ecstasy.
I have a box gift-wrapped and tied
With love to you, from me.

Color me soft and color me warm
In streams of pure delight.
Color me smiling at the end of day
In a radiant glowing life.

Color me friendly, in a state of bliss
In my sweet reverie.
No fantasies or silly myths,
But sweet reality.

My cup runs over, come stand in line.
Hold open your heart and mind.
Drink up, my friend, and come with me
To an endless joy divine.

The path of peace and happiness
And all that is good and true,
Is really lying very deep
Within the heart of you.

You are good, kind, charming and gay
In a basket of sweet joy sublime.
I color you happy too, my friend,
From now until the end of time.

II

Inspirations of Nature

From the Depths of Splendor

I find the richest pleasure
In the simple things of life;
In the cool of summer evenings,
In the dazzling starry nights;
In the rush of crystal water
Streaming down the mountainside;
Oh, the sweet breathtaking beauty
Seems to captivate my mind.

I would sink into the grandeur
And the splendor of it all,
Never daring to emerge
Lest I from, this wonder fall.
The sunset in the evening has
A splendor all its own and
I muse within my intellect,
Such wonder to behold.

The most wondrous thing I see
On the face of all the earth
Is the ocean, oh, so blue,
Rhapsodic grandeur tells its worth.
From the bottom of the ocean
Come the waves approaching land;
White with foam they kiss the seashore
And embrace the countless sands.

They dare not cross the threshold;
God has set a boundary there
And the multicolored rainbow
Speaks God's providential care.
Sea creatures safely nestled
In a colored waterbed,
Dare not leave protective shelter
But sink deeper down instead.

I see sunlight on the ocean,
Starry moon on midnight waves;
And it staggers all my senses,
Like the rolling of the waves.

I'm in a stupor as I gaze
Upon the ocean deep and wide;
I feel mystified with passion
And such ecstasy inside.

And from the depths of splendor
Raising my integrity,
I submit to God above me;
With my heart I dare believe.

I Ride the Deep

Oh, how I love the ocean blue,
Its power does not shirk.
Sometimes it lies so still, so still,
Then rises with a jerk.

The waves rush in to crash the shore,
I think I hear them speak;
Tide rushes in but soon lies down,
Then rolls back out to sea.

Oh, how I love the ocean blue,
The stormy winds will speak;
I cast my anchor through the waves,
Oh, yes, I ride the deep.

Sometimes my life is ocean blue,
So beautiful and so still,
Then the waves come crashing in,
To drown me if they will.

Tide rushes in but soon lies down,
And rolls back out to sea;
I cast my anchor through the waves,
Oh, yes, I ride the deep.

Water Symphony

I see the raindrops falling.
How they kiss my windowpane.
I hear the pitter patter and
Like a staccato quick refrain.

Like an orchestra so perfect,
Like a symphony so grand,
Bids me listen, bids me watch
God directing from His stand.

Like a symphony resounding
As the lightning cracks the sky,
The thunder renders echoes
Across the heavens wide.

Like stringed instruments in harmony,
The winds will play their part,
Humming, singing, whistling;
Their breath will travel far.

When this symphony has ended
And my mind seems mesmerized,
I remember the Creator;
He is directing from on high.

I Know the Storm Is Nigh

It's coming, it's coming—it's time, it's time,
I know that the storm is coming.
I wish there was somewhere I could go,
Sometimes I just feel like running.

Soon the rain fell, in the dark of the night,
Accompanied by great claps of thunder.
The lightning came and cracked the sky
And ripped many things asunder.

Oh, where could I go, where could I hide
From the greatness of God's power?
It's coming fast, so swift, so swift,
Treading down every minute and hour.

I heard God speak in the dark of the night;
Like a camera His lightning flashed,
Taking pictures of everything in view
And developed to a perfect match.

Sometimes even in the daylight hours,
Where no clouds appear in the sky,
I hear the sound of an austere wind,
And I know the storm is nigh.

The Wonder of Color

Yellow is the color of sunshine,
Green is the color of spring;
Joy is the song the robin sings
On the early morning wings.

The daffodils and the buttercups
Kiss the morning with a smile.
They dress the garden cheerfully
With elegance and style.

The rendezvous that follows
Is the quiet summer breeze.
Dancing winds with gentle sighs
Rush to kiss the willow trees.

The mixture of colors is the rainbow
After a steady and a sullen rain.
The sun peeps out from gray-clouded skies,
Making fun of the gloomy days.

This blanket of beauty is a painter's delight.
He absorbs the splendor it brings,
And captures sundown in a western sky,
Pink shadows now lift their wings.

In the Whisper of Sundown

In the whisper of sundown
Gentle breezes will blow;
In the late afternoon
Pink shadows will glow.

Rustling leaves on the trees
Wish to leave their abode
And dance across meadows
In a quick merry show.

In the whisper of sundown
The sky is so soft,
And sunset will capture
A golden hayloft.

In the whisper of sundown
When day is near done,
The cool summer breezes
Whisper, "Evening has begun."

Speak to Me Softly

Speak to me softly in the whisper of dawn,
Tell me that birds sing of day coming on.
Up, up—come on out, say hello to the sun,
Companion of day and friend to everyone.

The sun it arrives from an eastern sky,
Hushed is the song of the night lullaby.
Up, up—see the day how it moves so fast,
Soon the pouting night disappears at last.

The sky, how it draws me to capture its blue,
Invoking my praise to the One Artist True.
It is stretched as a canvas from east to west
And begins the day working to give its best.

Throughout the day few clouds will appear,
Their entrance not welcome, they soon disappear;
Shadows will fall, but pay them no mind,
The sun is in power and commands the daytime.

The sun he commands with conquering grin,
Shadows move back and fade as do whims.
Tell me this action is, oh, so grand?
The day is in power and covers the land.

Highways are crowded, there are busy city streets,
The day moves on, many people she greets.
They welcome her gladly, rejoice in her power,
The day will go on to linger for hours.

Afternoon and evening will quietly blend,
Turning to dusk, shaking hands with the wind.
City noises will mellow, traffic slows the town,
The day keeps working but soon will lie down.

The companion of day decides to rest,
Tucking his head far into the west.
The sun says to his daylight friend,
"We'll meet like this again, and again."

The evening gets weary, the night rushes in
And soon is caressed by soft-blowing winds.
The companions of night enter the scene and
Speak to me softly, saying, "Give heed."

The moon up high will command the night,
Thousands of stars will blink at his light.
They seem to wink at his half-sly grin and
Say to star gazers, we are all great friends.

The moon and stars appear as a cast,
Celebrity characters on stage at last.
But the curtain soon closes them out of sight
And away they all vanish into the night.

Speak to me softly in the whisper of dawn,
Tell me that birds sing of day coming on.
Up, up here he is, kiss the sun with a smile;
The day has returned for a long, long while.

III

Romance and Love

Our Eternal Love

Our love is like a ship sailing across a sea
that has no end.

Our love is like a dozen red roses;
their alluring beauty and fragrance
capture the senses of the beholder;

He is challenged to empty his purse and obtain
this personification of beauty and romance.

Our love is like Rhapsody in C Minor that is
splendidly played, then goes on to win the prize
for the most beautiful melody of our time.

You and I are held in the clutches of love's
sweet embrace that will not let us go.

Our love is entwined and aglow. Our love is like
one eternal flame that will not be quenched by the
rains of time.

Our love is forever and a day.

Our love survives.

Candlelight and You

The elegance of dining is
The candlelight, and you.
I revel in the evening with
Its amber-lighted view.

Soft music in the distance and
Fresh roses in the room,
Give a sweet and tender passion
To a night of love in bloom.

The warmth and sensual burning of
The candlelight is new and
Love is forever young in
Evening's twilight just for two.

No deeper words are spoken than
The three words "I love you,"
No feeling is so romantic as
The look that is shared by two.

The night is, oh, so young and
Tender love can't come too soon.
I cherish such sensation as
The candlelight, and you.

By the Fireside of Love

Could you begin to know my love,
The thoughts I have of thee?
I muse within my intellect of
Love's sweet mystery.

The look of love is in your eyes,
Thy smile is from above.
These tender thoughts I have of thee
By the fireside of love.

Thy touch sets me afire
And kindles high the flame,
Thy kisses are like honey drops;
My love for thee the same.

You stretch your hand to me
And I will surely come
Into your arms and warm embrace,
By the fireside of love.

I Wish You Love

I wish you springtime, sun and rain,
I wish you joy through all your pain.
May all your troubles dissipate?
I wish you love and never hate.

I wish you flowers in full bloom,
May sweet success come very soon?
I wish you sunlight from above,
But most of all I wish you love.

I wish you laughter through your tears,
I wish you peace throughout the year.
I wish you hope for a bright tomorrow,
From your dreams take time to borrow.

I wish you kindness on your way,
May mercy guide your path each day?
I wish you strength from up above,
But most of all I wish you love.

So Is My Love for Thee

Nothing can stop me from loving you,
Nor hinder my thoughts of care;
No mountain too high, or valley so low,
Not even the depths of despair.

Though bleak the sky and dark the night,
And endless at times it seems;
The dawning brings a brand new day,
So is my love for thee.

Plans may fail at any time and
Success is not guaranteed;
Yet sun, moon, and stars remain,
So is my love for thee.

Grass may wither and flowers fade;
Leaves may fade as a dream;
Children are born every minute each day,
So is my love for thee.

The look of love is in your eyes.
Deep within my heart I see,
Eternity—it has no end,
So is my love for thee.

Intoxicated Over You

My heart goes pitter patter over you;
My mind is in a whirlwind stirred anew;
My thoughts just drift about me and
I am dazzled by your charm;
I am so intoxicated over you.

Look at me and suddenly my heart will sing
Melodies of true romance and lovely dreams.
I can't help but really love you,
I can't help the way that I feel;
I am so intoxicated over you.

You speak in tones so soft and words are new;
You say to me, "I love you" and it's true;
You're my knight in shining armor;
I am queen within your world;
I am so intoxicated over you.

I am staggered at your power over me;
Your love is like none other I have known;
You're my lover and friend, the man I call my own;
I am so intoxicated over you.

The Way I Love You

I love you on a quiet afternoon and
In the twilight of the evening.

I love you in the still of the night and
In the whisper of dawn.

I love you with the heat of passion in
Summer, and in the soft blowing winds of autumn.

I love you with the ecstasy of midnight
Breezes along the ocean front, and in
The splendor under a moonlit sky.

I love you in the crispness of winter and
In the freshness of spring.

I love you in stormy weather and
Also in the downpour of rain.

I love you through laughter and tears,
Even more in the aftermath of a storm.

I love you with every waking moment of
Each new day.

I love you with all of my heart and soul,
With my mind and body.

I love you with every fiber of my being, and
Within the realms of my intellect.

IV

Spiritual
Insights

Thy Will, O Lord, Be Done

When clouds dim the skies
And troubled waters arise,
And my battle is yet to be won,
I ask God to give me strength to say
Thy will, O Lord, be done.

Swift waters run deep,
Mine eyes do weep;
It's dark and I can't see the sun.
I ask God to give me strength to say
Thy will, O Lord, be done.

God stands at the helm while
My heart is overwhelmed
In the midst of a high, rising flood.
He heard me pray, gave me strength to say
Thy will, O Lord, be done.

Let Excellence Reign

Let excellence reign
In the heart of man;
Let it sit on the throne,
Let it be in command.

Like kings in great splendor,
Like chariots of gold,
Let excellence ride,
Take control of the soul.

Let the path that it trods
Have a light shining bright;
Let the pace be smooth,
Never turning from right.

Like kings on thrones
Robed in grand array;
His excellence reigns;
Jesus Christ is His Name!

Launch Out
(*Luke 8:22–25*)

Get on board, get on board,
For the ship must sail.
Winds may be contrary,
But you will not fail.

Launch out and sail
To the other side;
Dare to cross the wide sea
And sail with the tide.

Launch out, launch out
Into the deep,
Even though your Master
Seems fast asleep;

Asleep in your life?
Do you fear the high tide?
Wake up your Master,
He will hear when you cry.

Though you're tossed to and fro
On the sea of life,
If you will just call,
He will quickly arise.

He will speak to the winds,
Just watch them subside;
Give you peace deep within;
He abides, He abides.

Beyond the Horizon

I see the rainbow in the sky,
Put there for me and you
And I look beyond the horizon
Far beyond the sky of blue.

I rise above earth's atmosphere,
Through floating clouds I see
And soar above the elements
On wings of faith and peace.

I fly straight into the sun,
Leaving shadows far behind
And muse within my intellect,
This universe far and wide.

God's promise always will remain,
His word is ever true.
So I look beyond the horizon,
Far beyond the sky of blue.

Someday

Someday we will rise above this world,
See heaven and all of its beauty unfurled.
Jewels, precious jewels our eyes shall behold,
Yes, rapturous beauty, the half yet untold.

Someday our troubles unfamiliar will be,
We will not know sorrow, but peace and harmony;
Never tire of singing or giving God praise,
Hallelujah! The Lord God Omnipotent reigns.

Heaven must be a wonderful place,
With mystical minds, this thought we embrace.
So now let us run with patience this race,
Someday we will rise and behold Jesus' face.

Memories, They Are the Dreams

Memories, they are the dreams
That vanish into night,
And strive to keep them as I may,
They soon drift out of sight.

Yet I recall these fading dreams
Into my intellect;
For dreams without a memory
Are often quite suspect.

A new dream on the threshold
Waiting to invade my mind
Is color-coded just for me,
It's clear, it is fresh and bright.

I'm dreaming far beyond the blue
To a morning just begun.
It is the breaking of the day,
I'm looking at the sun.

Think on These Things
(*Phil. 4:7–8*)

Keep your mind on Jesus, peace He will give,
And o'er troubled waters, He'll be your bridge.
Set all your affection on things above,
In faith believing that God is love.

If you expect to leave this earth,
Your mind must dwell on things of worth,
The kingdom of God and His righteousness;
His power and grace through His Son Jesus.

Think on things that are honest, just and true,
Pure and lovely and whatever is good.
Go into the vineyard and work today
And whatever is right God will pay.

Cords of Love
(*Ezek. 16:1–9*)

I was not washed in water
In the day that I was born.
I was not swaddled, not at all,
No one could cut the cord.

No one would dare to pity me,
Or show to me compassion.
Polluted was I in my own blood,
They hated me with a passion.

They cast me out in the open field,
Attached was I to sin.
God passed by and looked at me
And said to me, "Child live!"

God looked at me in my condition,
Polluted deep in my blood.
With cords of love He drew me
And rescued me from the flood.

Open Mine Eyes

Open mine eyes that I might see
More of life's great mystery.
Let me find the key to happiness,
The path of peace and blessedness.

Give me a vision, let me see the well
And I will then a story tell.
When I am tempted to give up,
Come, Lord Jesus, fill my cup.

Let me perceive Thy glory, Lord,
Give to me Thy golden Word.
Show me the invisible brought to light;
I'll cling to the vision with all my might.

Awaken my mind to righteousness,
Attend my soul, I shall be blessed.
Open mine eyes to reality and I will
See a glimpse of eternity.

O God, Your Love Is Constant

O God, Your Love is constant,
Your faithfulness is great,
Your mercy I receive each day,
On this I meditate.

Your love, it is not foreign,
I embrace it every day;
Sufficient is Your grace for me,
I truly am amazed.

You come to me whenever I call,
For I must be set free;
With hand outstretched to lift me up,
You draw me close to Thee.

Oh, never shall I doubt you Lord,
Each morning when I wake
I look up to the open sky
And give to You my praise.

O God, your love is constant,
Your faithfulness is great,
No one can love me like You, Lord;
No one can take Your place.

May God Bless All His Children

May God bless all His children,
Red and yellow, black and white?
May they learn to love each other?
May they cease from all their strife?

May God bless all His children,
Young and old, the great and small?
Let undying love enfold them;
From His grace let them never fall.

May cruel envy disappear?
And let hatred hide its head.
May God's love enrich all lives,
And let goodness crown each head?

Cherish the Children

Cherish the children, give them your heart,
They enter this world with a brand new start.
Look at the beauty in their sparkling eyes,
Bundles of energy and the spices of life.

Hear their laughter and the sounds of joy,
Give them more love and less of the toys.
Their inquiring minds will seek to know,
Give them an answer and let them grow.

Cherish the children and show your concern,
Teach them early God's holy word.
Instruct them in wisdom and teach them to pray,
Love them with passion and be ready to save.

Let them laugh, play, and sing all day long,
Instruct them in knowledge of right from wrong.
They will grow up and reflect in life's mirror
And cherish their children down through the years.

Gifts of Life

Give me sunlight in the morning
And great shade trees at high noon,
Give me quiet winds at evening,
In the night give me the moon.

Give me violins and roses,
Serenade me with a song;
Whisper in my ear sweet nothings
That I'll dream of all night long.

Give me daffodils and buttercups
And roses in full bloom,
Give me violets and tulips
And the morning glories too.

Give me robins as they sing
With the early morning dew;
Give me rain and grass so green,
And a sky of heavenly blue.

Give me children and their laughter,
Many girls and many boys;
Give me tiny newborn babies,
How they fill my heart with joy.

Give me people, I love people,
Send Your Spirit from above;
Fill each heart with Thy great peace
And undying boundless love.

Give me strength throughout the night,
Give me grace to walk with Thee;
Give me wisdom, give me light;
I will give You all of me.

I'm Black But Comely

My skin is dark and my bones are strong,
My mind is clear and I'm moving on.
I'm black but comely, don't look down on me,
God made me this lovely, God made me free.

I've known toil and sweat in the heat of the day,
The sun beat upon me, I longed for the shade.
I've known sorrow, agony, and the pains of life;
I struggle to cope in a world full of strife.

I was down so very long, and knew only to frown
But I'm getting up now, a smile is coming 'round.
You look at me and see imperfections;
I'm black but comely, it's my introspection.

I've worked for others, slaved at their command,
I'm black but comely, and I still have a plan.
I can do anything I want, for it's firm in my mind,
To make it rain in the desert, or snow in July.

I've my wits about me, I'm wise don't you see?
No more chains, no more chains, at last I am free.
I've felt many whips and have stripes on my back,
But surely I'm healing, it's a well-known fact.

You think I've no sense, like an animal that is dumb,
But I'm wise don't you see, I've risen from the dung?
In the pursuit of life, liberty and happiness,
I remain black but comely; I'm proud, I confess.

I've increased in wisdom and acquired great gain,
God saw my position and gave retribution for my pain.
So travel from afar, come and inquire about me,
I'm black but comely, and God made me.

I Fell Right into Your Grace

I've fallen down, that is what I said,
Such shame was on my face;
I looked around and to my surprise,
I fell right into Your grace.

I've fallen down and I confess
That I missed the mark today.
Some may judge me to be lost,
But I fell right into Your grace.

Some criticized and passed me by;
They whispered "What a waste."
But they failed to see Your loving hand,
When I fell right into Your grace.

I've fallen down, that is what I said,
But I will get up today.
Oh, how could I ever doubt You, Lord
When I fell right into Your grace?

Looking for God

I've traveled the highways and byways of life,
Looking for God to come into my life.
I've ridden trailways through tunnels deep and wide;
I've drifted o'er waters and sailed seas of time.

I wandered in the forest and viewed the pine trees,
I sauntered through thickets and trampled the leaves.
I roamed through the valley where multitudes trod,
I climbed hills and mountains, looking for God.

I left this old earth and soared through the air
And viewed God's creation in beauty so rare.
Down, down I descended again,
Gliding I went back to earth's vast domain.

I ventured one day into the House of Prayer,
Still looking and hoping I might find God there.
I bended my knees at the altar of God;
I humbled myself, how my heart did throb.
I had only to believe and open my eyes,
For all that time I spent searching,
God was right there inside.

The Fool
(*Luke 12:16–21*)

"Heaven and Hell are here on earth,"
The fool says in his heart,
"I'll live and do anyway that I please
'Til from this life I part."

He says to his soul, "Thou hast much goods
Laid up for many years,
Take thine ease, eat, drink and be merry
For thou hast nothing to fear."

The fool he eats, he drinks and is merry,
"There is no God" says he.
But God said to him, "Thou fool, this night
Thy soul is required of thee."

It's appointed to men once to die
And after death the judgment,
So live and do—anyway you please;
Remember your days are numbered.

The Prodigal
(*Luke 15:11–24*)

Oh, wanderer, wanderer, where did you go?
Seeking the kingdoms in valleys so low;
Searching for pleasures and riches of men;
You had everything in the country of kin.

Food, clothing, and riches were many;
Shelter secure and servants were plenty;
All this and more—abundance untold;
You went from the mountain to valleys so low.

Oh, wanderer, wanderer, where did you go?
Far, far away to spend all thy gold;
You had no care for the one you did leave
'Til you sank in the gutter, now his mercy you plead.

Get up, get up, wallow not in self-pity
For wasting your life on a faraway city.
Get up, get up, from the valleys so low;
Oh, wanderer, wanderer, come back to the fold.

The Crying Heart

Last night I cried as though one died,
The pain seemed great to bear
And for yet a while I lost my smile,
Am I alone to care?

Can I speak to One who will understand
All the things I want to say
About people discouraged and in despair
Who turn to walk away?

Away from God and His tender care
And protection of His fold,
Away from His love and warmth of light
Into the night so cold.

Sometimes I wish I could not care
Because of all the pain,
But then my heart would be so hard
And life would seem in vain.

So I spill out my heart—the waters run down
And color the mountainside.
These tears flow quickly into rivers deep
And my heart is overwhelmed inside.

And deep within me I would burst
And sometimes think escape
From all of life's care and many worries,
How much precious time they take.

But God will mend this broken heart
Because He always cares.
He'll mend every rip with great precision,
You will see a fine repair.

Your Honor

Jesus of Nazareth, Thou Son of David,
How precious, how precious Thou art.
Like bright rays of sunlight
In each new day dawning
And music played softly on harps.

So rich art Thou, Lord, in Thy great love,
And mercy renewed every morning.
Like dew drops on flowers shining as jewels;
I cherish Thy beauty adorning.

How can I tell Thee how wondrous Thou art?
The praise, how it muses within
The realm of my intellect and innermost being
My soul says Amen and Amen.

Let me walk with Thee, Jesus, and linger forever,
Your Honor this is the request that I'm
Asking of Thee, may it please your Majesty?
For with Thee I'm eternally blessed.

Unequaled
(*Isaiah 40:12–18*)

Who measured the water in the Hollow of His hand?
Who meted out the heavens with a span?
Who comprehended the dust of the earth in measure, or
Weighed the mountains in scales; who reigns forever?

Who directs the Lord or counsels Him?
Who teaches Him in paths of judgment?
Who instructs the Lord or teaches Him knowledge?
Whom will you compare to His likeness?

Oh, islands keep silent, bow down thine heads
And fall down prostrate at His feet.
The Alpha and Omega, Beginning and Ending;
Omnipotent Ruler, He speaks!

Like a drop in a bucket are the nations to God.
They are counted as vanity.
They spring forth like flowers and new blades of grass
And like vapors they vanish away.

On the Rampage

Death is on the rampage,
Death is on your trail,
Moving fast at God's command
So cry, lament, bewail!

He mounts the horse, a pale horse;
I've watched him for a while,
Marking time, prancing, trotting
Until God says, "Go your miles!"

The pale white horse, he picks up speed
From a trot to a heavy gallop.
He triumphs, conquers hills and mountains,
So cry but you can't stop him.

The pale white horse and his rider move on;
You're in the path, watch out!
He'll snatch you from life, take you away,
You will ride, this horse you will mount.

The pale white horse with leaping strides
Comes knocking at your door.
So ignore and don't answer, or give a care,
He will enter the house of yours.

The Dream

There's a dream running by,
Swiftly passing to the sky.
You dreamed it, did you not?
'Twas embedded in your thoughts,
In your heart and in your mind,
A dream that there will be no time.

Such requited love and joy,
Happiness without alloy
Is the center of the dream if you
Are washed and have been redeemed.
Yes, you're dreaming like us all,
All the saints both great and small.

It's in your heart and in your mind,
A dream that there will be no time.
But, oh, then something else will be;
That something is called eternity.
God split eternity in two,
Just for me and just for you.

Time fills this far and reaching space;
We call it God's amazing grace!
God gave us time to laugh and cry;
To sing and pray, to live and die;
To be saved and sin no more;
To worship Him, His Name adore.

God gave us space, a space of time,
But between eternity we find
The space is getting short,
Getting shorter, getting shorter,
Eternity is coming back together,
My dream, your dream is coming true.

It's in your heart and in your mind,
A dream that there will be no time.
And like the dream that's running by
Swiftly passing to the sky,
We'll find the dream is a reality;
We are there at home, on high.

Rich Man—Poor Man
(*Luke 16:19–29*)

Rich man, poor man, beggar man, or thief,
The poor seeks daily a little relief.
To the rich he prays, "A crumb, please spare
That I may get along on meager fare?
I'd lay my weary head down upon my bed
If I could only have, but a piece of bread."

The poor man's clothes are tattered and torn,
His body aches from all the sores.
He lays at the gate both day and night,
The dog licks his sores, such a pitiful sight.
He is down so low in a dismal night;
Will God in heaven turn this wrong into right?

The rich man scorns, the poor is despised,
The high and mighty walk a very thin line.
They too will come to the depths of despair
For keeping their bounty and refusing to share
Not a piece of bread, not even a crumb,
But quickly turn, from the poor they run.

The rich man and poor man, both of them died
And passed from life to the other side.
The rich left his wealth and his golden bed;
I wonder now, where he will lay his head?
His rubies and diamonds, his wealth untold,
In sorrow he kept, in exchange for his soul.

The rich looked up from the depths of Hell,
And the poor man in heaven sang, "All is well."
Now tell me who is the one seeking relief?
Rich man, poor man, beggar man, or thief?
They both sought relief in a frame called time,
The poor when he lived, the rich when he died.

I'll tell you of Hannah who prayed and said,
"The Lord lifts up the bowed down head.
God fills the hungry, his soul He feeds.
The rich are sent away, God's mercy they plead.
The rich are tormented in a terrible flame,
The poor have comfort and freedom from pain."

"Don't talk so proud," dear Hannah prayed,
"The God of knowledge has your actions weighed.
How the mighty are fallen, in shame they lay;
The poor are brought up, from the dust they are raised."
Death comes to both the rich and poor alike
And God in His wisdom makes all things right.

I've Also Cried Rivers of Joy

I have had sorrow and pain, even strife,
Disappointments often invaded my life.
Oh, I have cried rivers of misery,
But I've also cried rivers of joy.

I've cried over people, and certain things,
Even cried all night long for trouble they bring.
There were days when I just couldn't get along
Without feeling my world had turned upside down.

I had some pity parties and said, "Woe is me,
For nobody knows the trouble I've seen."
But self-pity is wrong, I thought one day and
Mused in my intellect, God will make a way.

He took my burden, replaced it with a song,
Made everything right and chased away wrong.
Skies are not always cloudy and gray;
The sun is not hiding, it just traveled away.

I've had days when things looked so bright,
God was in his Heaven, all the world was right.
I soared like an eagle and took to the skies;
I came, I saw, and I conquered the night.

So I can face sorrow and pain, even strife
And handle disappointments invading my life.
Oh, I have cried rivers of misery,
But I've also cried rivers of joy.

V

In Loving Memory

Memories of those I have loved so dear
Will forever stay in my mind,
Like the lingering fragrance of sweet perfume,
Like the rainbow in the sky after summer rain,
Like the afterglow of the sun in a western sky.

Out of the Waters
(*In Loving Memory of my brother, Danny*)

God poured me out into the deep
And there but for a while,
From the depths of the sea I quickly arose
And faced Him with a smile.

He said, "I'm God, Creator of life
And Maker of all you see,
Oh come dear one return thyself,
Return thyself to Me."

He drew me out of the waters of life
And led me to a shore,
Angels sang, "You are home dear one,
Return to the sea no more.

" 'Tis a better place for thee, my son;
The winds are sweet and new;
God has sent the ship back out to sea
And others will follow you."

Danny boy, sweet Danny boy,
You sank into the deep,
God drew you out of the waters of life,
Now in His arms you are free.

Danny boy, sweet Danny boy,
My thoughts, they follow thee;
These tears I'll drop and later board
That same ship on the sea.

For I am poured out into the deep
And there but for a while,
God will draw me out where winds are new,
I'll face Him with a smile.

Drifting Out to Sea
(*In Loving Memory of my brother, Buddy*)

My Buddy, how I loved him,
Though very far from me;
I looked, I searched, and then
I found him drifting out to sea.

Such a slender frame was Buddy,
Dark and tender-eyed was he,
And water streaming from his eyes
Has quickly flowed to sea.

Home is where he wants to go,
The place from which he came.
He travels back a different route,
It's easier this way.

My Buddy, you have left me,
But I'll see you in my dreams.
I am standing on the bank and
You are drifting out to sea.

Your ship now vanishing from sight
Will not return to me;
And water streaming from my eyes
Will flow out to your sea.

Thy soul to God thy Maker,
Thy spirit He will receive.
He will escort you safe on shore;
God will remember thee.

I'll Always Love You, Mama
(*In Loving Memory of my beautiful mother*)

I'll always love you, Mama,
I love you now, it's true;
And when I look up to the sky,
I often think of you.

Within my heart I see you,
My love for you remains;
I long to see your smiling face
And touch your slender hands.

So beautiful and quiet,
That's how I remember you,
I see your face and behold your smile;
I can hear you singing too.

You were so very beautiful,
You still are in my heart.
Because my love remains for you,
We're never far apart.

I'll always love you, Mama,
I love you now, it's true;
You cannot come again to me,
But I shall come to you.

Like a Dream
(*Written in route to my husband's Home Going—*
August 5, 2002—10:50 A.M.)

Like a dream you vanished into night,
And you will soon wake up in the day.
Like a dream you vanished out of sight,
Still I can see you anyway.

This dream was long, so very long,
Our dream was very bright.
I will see you very soon, my love,
In the early morning Light.

It was suddenly that I lost you;
You disappeared from my sight.
And when I wake up from this dream,
I will find you in the Light.

We are in this dream together,
And I will vanish into night.
And I will soon wake up in the day,
In God's Eternal Light.

                                          Forever Yours,
                                          Carol